D1016114

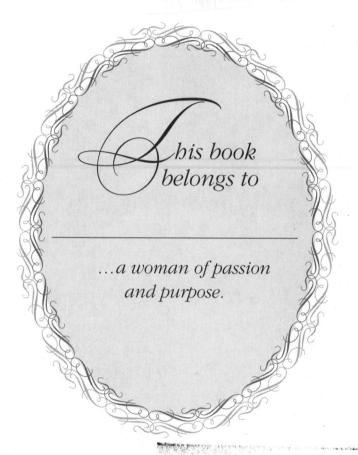

*T*his book
belongs to

_____

...*a woman of passion
and purpose.*

Life Management for Busy Women

GROWTH AND STUDY GUIDE

Elizabeth George

HARVEST HOUSE™PUBLISHERS

EUGENE, OREGON

Cover by Terry Dugan Design, Minneapolis, Minnesota

Acknowledgment

As always, thank you to my dear husband, Jim George, M.Div., Th.M., for your able assistance, guidance, suggestions, and loving encouragement on this project.

Contents

A Word of Welcome

Please let me welcome you to this fun (and stretching!) growth and study guide for women like you who desire to truly, passionately, and purposefully live out God's plan for your life. I know you're frightfully busy, but as you take the time to apply the guidelines and disciplines discussed in this study, you'll discover how glorious a better-managed life can be.

A Word of Instruction

To do the exercises in this study guide, you'll need your copy of the book *Life Management for Busy Women*, and your Bible, a pen, a dictionary, and a heart ready to grow. In each lesson you'll be asked to:

✓ Read the corresponding chapter from *Life Management for Busy Women*.

✓ Answer the questions designed to guide you to greater spiritual growth and better life management.

✓ Write out a workable plan for the upcoming days of your life that incorporates the guidelines and disciplines discussed in your lesson.

5

A Word to Your Group

Of course, you can grow (volumes!) as you work your way alone through these truths from God's Word and apply them to your busy life. But I urge you to share the journey with other women. A group, no matter how small or large, offers personal care and interest. There is sharing. There are sisters-in-Christ to pray for you. There is the mutual exchange of experiences. There is accountability. And, yes, there is peer pressure, which always helps us get our lessons done! And there is sweet, sweet encouragement as together you stimulate one another to greater love and greater works of love (Hebrews 10:24).

To aid the woman who is guided by God to lead a group, I've included a section in the back of this growth and study book called "Leading a Bible Study Discussion Group."

A Word of Encouragement

If you will use the insights, tools, and how-to's gained from the book *Life Management for Busy Women* and from this study guide, by God's grace and with His help, the passion and purpose that exudes from the life of a woman who truly lives out God's plan will become yours. Your ways will glorify Him. Managing anything is work...especially managing a busy life! But, dear one, as you "work" your way *through* this life-changing study, and as you "work" God's plan *into* your life, you'll be pleasantly surprised as suddenly the meaningless peripherals "work" their way *out* of your life! And then there will be time...time to enjoy the deep peace that comes from knowing that you are managing your life God's way.

1

Developing a Passion
for God's Word

But those who wait on the LORD shall renew their strength;
they shall mount up with wings like eagles, they shall run
and not be weary, they shall walk and not faint.
—ISAIAH 40:31

 Begin this lesson by reading the chapter in *Life Management for Busy Women* titled "Developing a Passion for God's Word." Note here any new truths or challenges that stand out to you.

I shared with you some of my first waking thoughts each morning when my alarm clock goes off. Now, share a few of yours.

Now read John 15:4-5. What truths does verse 4 teach us about managing our lives?

And what truths does verse 5 teach?

As you think about these two verses and their messages to us, what can you conclude regarding managing your spiritual life?

Like an Eagle

Look now at Isaiah 40:30-31. Note the condition of "the youth" and "the young men" in verse 30.

What happens by contrast to "those who wait on the LORD" (verse 31)?

—

—

—

—

Three Small Steps

1. *Time*—Do you AGREE or DISAGREE that time spent with the Lord in His Word is always time well spent (circle one)? Take a minute to reflect on the past few weeks. Have you spent time in God's Word? About how often? About how much time per day? Per week? What changes must you make to spend time each day reading your Bible?

2. *First* time—Think back to a time when you spent the *first* minutes of your day reading your Bible. What difference did meeting with God first thing make in your day?

3. *Early* time—First things first! We know meeting with God each day is the most important thing a busy woman can do to manage her life. And early seems to be the key! How did these busy people accomplish meeting with God?

—Abraham (Genesis 19:27)

—David (Psalm 5:3)

—Jesus (Mark 1:35)

Your time—What time do you normally get up?

What time does your family normally get up?

For you to get up a little earlier to ensure *time, first* time, and *early* time with God, what time would you need to get up to have *your* time?

Would you be willing to get up at the time you just indicated for five days (Monday through Friday) so that you, too, regardless of your busy-ness, can soar with passion and purpose like an eagle through your packed, fast-track days?

I'm assuming your answer is *yes*. So I want you to check off those days you get up a little early in the coming week. Then take a minute to write out something about the time you spent in God's Word. What did you discover? What ministered to you? How did your time prepare you for the day?

Monday_____

Tuesday_____

Wednesday_____

Thursday_____

Friday_____

The Power of God's Word

God's Word is the heart of God—What do these scriptures teach us about God's Word and His heart?

—2 Timothy 3:16

—Psalm 33:11

God's Word is a good use of your time—What word is used in 2 Timothy 3:16 to describe this fact?

God's Word teaches you—Look at the Bible's description of "silly women" in 2 Timothy 3:6-7 (KJV). What was their dilemma?

Now read verse 16. How is the Word of God the solution?

God's Word reproves you—What many active roles are attributed to the Word of God in Hebrews 4:12?

What active roles are attributed to the Word of God in 2 Timothy 3:16?

God's Word corrects, mends, and instructs you—Can you share a truth from the Bible that recently corrected and instructed your behavior? (If you can't think of an instance, look at Proverbs 15:1 and share how this verse could correct and instruct any woman!)

God's Word equips you—According to 2 Timothy 3:17, what does the Word of God do for you?

Can you share a verse that never fails to build you up for the tasks God has given you? (If you can't think of a verse, share how Philippians 4:13 encourages and and equips you...just for today.)

God's Word guides you—Are there decisions you need to make? Does the unknown path ahead of you sometimes seem dark and mysterious? How can God's Word help, according to Psalm 119:105?

God's Word cheers you—What role did the Word of God play in Jeremiah's hard, sad, and lonely life (Jeremiah 15:16)?

In your times of sadness, learn to turn to God's Word! Do you have a favorite verse or truth that brings you instant cheer? (If you can't think of any, how does Hebrews 13:5 cheer you…just for today?)

Passion for anything—including God's Word—is not developed in a moment, but in a sustained involvement for months or even years. Dear one, develop a passion for God's Word that is sustained over the years…and then God's Word will sustain you over the years.

~ *The Bible* ~

The Bible contains…
>   the mind of God.
>   the state of man.
>   the way of salvation.
>   the doom of sinners.
>   the happiness of believers.
>   light to direct you.
>   food to support you.
>   comfort to cheer you.

It is…
>   the traveler's map.
>   the pilgrim's staff.
>   the pilot's compass.
>   the soldier's sword.
>   the Christian's charter.
>   a mine of wealth.
>   a paradise of glory.
>   a river of pleasure.

You should…
>   read it to be wise.
>   believe it to be safe.
>   practice it to be holy.

It should…
>   fill the memory.
>   rule the heart.
>   guide the feet.[1]

Looking at Your Life

Please read the "Looking at Life" section in your book again. As you consider the management of your busy life in the light of the contents of this chapter, what actions do you plan to take to live out God's plan for your spiritual life…

…just for today?

…just for this week?

…just for this month?

…just for this year?

…for life?

2

Ten Disciplines for Developing
a Passion for God's Word

I have treasured the words of His mouth
more than my necessary food.
—JOB 23:12

 Begin this lesson by reading the chapter in *Life Management for Busy Women* titled "Ten Disciplines for Developing a Passion for God's Word." Note here any new truths or challenges that stand out to you.

As a beginning exercise, look up the word *discipline* in a dictionary and write out the meaning here. Then write out the definition in your own words.

Ten Disciplines for Developing a Passion for God's Word

1. *Refuse to miss a day*—How are you doing on the commitment you made in our previous lesson to spend time in God's Word each day?

   How important did Job think God's Word was (Job 23:12)?

   Beginning with this lesson, use the Quiet Times Calendar at the end of the book for recording your progress in this discipline of refusing to miss a day.

2. *Pray as you approach God's Word*—For what did these three people of God desire concerning God's Word?

   —the psalmist in Psalm 119:18-19?

   —Solomon in Proverbs 2:2-3?

   —the apostle Paul in Colossians 3:16?

   —and you? For what will you pray?

17

3. *Consume God's Word in various ways*—Think through the various ways mentioned in your lesson. Then talk to others to discover some of the many ways they enjoy God's Word. What new way(s) for consuming God's Word will you try, and how will you get set up?

4. *Find a rhythm or a pattern that fits your lifestyle*—Are there any wrinkles in your lifestyle that you may be allowing to keep you from reading your Bible? For instance, do you, perhaps like the young mom in the letter, let the little ones keep you from the most important thing (having your quiet time) you must do each day? Or do you have a job…and there just doesn't seem to be time to stop and linger awhile with the Lord before you dash out the door? Or are you a little on the lazy side and just never seem to get around to it? Name your greatest obstacle…and then write out what you can…and will…do to find a rhythm or pattern that fits your lifestyle so you can develop a passion for God's Word.

5. *Be a woman of one Book—the Book*—Now take a minute to think through your reading habits. What do you tend to read most? About how many minutes a day do you read? As you weigh this amount of time against the number of minutes you spend each day reading your Bible, how do things stack up? Is the scale tilted…or does your reading indicate that you are a woman of one Book—the Book? Are there any changes you need to make? If so, what?

Revisit the "Rules for Daily Life" at the end of chapter 2 and then...

> *Open the book of God*
> And read a portion there;
> That it may hallow all thy thoughts,
> And sweeten all thy care.

6. *Be accountable*—As a Christian you are a member of a body of believers, the church, the body of Christ. And other Christians can be of valuable help to you by holding you accountable for your spiritual growth...but you must ask! Read Titus 2:3-5. God has given every Christian woman a dual role—she is to teach (or mentor) others, and she is to be taught (or mentored) by others. This teaching and mentoring ministry is accountability in action. Now, as you think of the three groups of friends mentioned in your book, list the friends you have in your church who pull you along and older women who can pull you up.

What steps will you take to become more accountable for developing the discipline of faithfulness in your quiet time? Or, put another way, *who* will you ask to help you?

7. *Beat the family*—As I said, this may sound strange! But by getting up each morning before the family gets up, you make time for the most important thing you will do all day! And once you've *received* from the Father what you need for your day by reading His Word, you will then have what your dear family and others need to *receive* from you all day long. Now, *how* can you make this discipline a reality?

8. *Teach your children*—Read now Deuteronomy 6:5-7. What does this passage say about...

...your love for the Lord?

...your heart?

...your role as a mother?

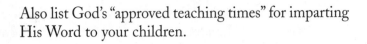

Also list God's "approved teaching times" for imparting His Word to your children.

—

—

—

—

Now, what is your plan for working this important role into your busy schedule?

9. *Purpose to get up*—I'm sure it seems like I'm hammering away on this one discipline...and I am! But it's vital! Getting up is key to managing any and every area of your life. So purpose to get up tomorrow and for the rest of the week. Then recount your many blessings and your increased passion. (And I'm sure this space isn't long enough! So just share a few.)

10. *Aim for more time*—Write out the two principles for determining the amount of time you spend reading your Bible.

—

—

How do you think these two do-able principles can help you have success in your desire to daily spend time in God's Word?

As you contemplate the closing section of this chapter and Edith Schaeffer's thought that "life is a mountain climb to the very end," where do you consider yourself to be on that mountain climb?

And how do you think the disciplines for consuming God's Word will (and did!) assist you in your passion for your climb?

For top performance we must
refuel daily from the Word.

Looking at Your Life

Please read the "Looking at Life" section in your book again. As you consider the management of your busy life in the light of the contents of this chapter, what actions do you plan to take to live out God's plan for your spiritual life...

...just for today?

...just for this week?

...just for this month?

...just for this year?

...for life?

Developing a Passion for Prayer

My voice You shall hear in the morning, O LORD;
in the morning I will direct it to You, and I will look up.
—PSALM 5:3

Begin this lesson by reading the chapter in *Life Management for Busy Women* titled "Developing a Passion for Prayer." Note here any new truths or challenges that stand out to you.

Our Call to Prayer

As we head into this vital study about the importance of nurturing a passion for prayer, look first at these verses from the Bible and write out what they have to say about our call to prayer.

Jeremiah 33:3—

Matthew 6:6—

Matthew 7:7—

James 1:5—

Prayer is a privilege—What do these scriptures teach us
   about the privilege of prayer?
   —Psalm 34:17-18

   —Psalm 145:18

   —Hebrews 4:16

   —1 Peter 3:12

What is the condition of your heart and your life at this time? Do you need to exercise your privilege and call out to God in prayer?

Prayer nurtures our trust in God—How do these scriptures indicate reasons to trust in God?

—Psalm 5:3

—Matthew 7:11

What obvious action do these verses call for on your part in nurturing a deeper trust in God?

Prayer guides us in the path of righteousness—How do these scriptures indicate our need for God's guidance?

—Proverbs 14:12

—Jeremiah 17:9

—James 4:3

The act of prayer surfaces and purifies our motives. What decisions are you facing that you need to take to God in prayer?

Prayer assists our relationship with God—Read these three accounts of men who prayed to God and note how prayer assisted their relationships with God.

—David in Psalm 32:1-5

—David in Psalm 51:1-4,12

—Samson in Judges 16:23-31

Is there any unconfessed sin you should pray about so that your joy and usefulness is restored?

Prayer strengthens us against our tendency to sin—Here are three common scenarios that tempt us to sin. What is the problem and what is the solution in each instance?

—Matthew 5:44

—Mark 11:25

—Philippians 4:6-7

Are you struggling with a problem...or problem-person? How do you think prayer would strengthen you to handle the problem God's way?

How Then Should We Pray?

Consider each of the practical instructions below that teach us *how* we are to pray. Note what the scriptures have to say about each practice.

• We should pray respectfully—Isaiah 55:8-9

• We should pray regularly—Matthew 6:5-7

• We should (and can) learn to pray—Luke 11:1

• We should pray humbly—Luke 18:10-14

• We should pray broadly—Ephesians 6:18

• We should pray boldly—Hebrews 4:16

Which of these practices are already present in your prayer life? And which are missing?

Getting Down to the Disciplines

1. *Make a commitment*—Now it's your turn to make a commitment to be more faithful in prayer. You may write it in the back of this growth and study guide, in the back of your book, or in your prayer journal or notebook. Wherever you write it, be sure you save it. It's an important, revolutionary, life-changing commitment! (Check here when done.) _____

2. *Realize that prayer is not optional*—Note the depth and breadth of prayer indicated in Ephesians 6:18.

    When are we to pray?

    How are we to pray?

    Who are we to pray for?

3. *Refuse to miss a day*—Life is filled with daily challenges. Therefore we should pray every day to meet those challenges head-on. Write out again the two principles that can help you develop the discipline of daily prayer.

    —

    —

4. *Study the prayers of the Bible*—To get started on this invaluable exercise, read through these prayers.

    —Ephesians 1:15-19

    —Ephesians 3:14-21

    —Colossians 1:9-14

5. *Study the prayers of the saints through the ages*—I hope you find some wonderful volumes of inspiring prayers prayed by others. For now, enjoy this one from Susanna Wesley regarding her own prayer time:

> May no slight access of trouble have power to ruffle my temper, and to indispose or distract my mind in my addresses to heaven, in reading, meditation or any other spiritual exercise.[2]

One more thing—how do you think praying about each activity of your life would keep you from "majoring on the minors"?

Hopefully by now you realize that the Bible and prayer are at the heart of a busy woman's management of her life. What Jesus said is true—"Without me you can do nothing" (John 15:5).

Life management begins with
managing your prayer life.

Looking at Your Life

Please read the "Looking at Life" section in your book again. As you consider the management of your busy life in the light of the contents of this chapter, what actions do you plan to take to live out God's plan for your spiritual life...

...just for today?

...just for this week?

...just for this month?

...just for this year?

...for life?

4

God's Guidelines
for Your Body

Your body is the temple of the Holy Spirit.
—1 CORINTHIANS 6:19

Begin this lesson by reading the chapter in *Life Management for Busy Women* titled "God's Guidelines for Your Body." Note here any new truths or challenges that stand out to you.

I shared some personal reasons for making the management of my physical life a high priority. Now share a few of yours.

Your Body Is a Temple

Look at 1 Corinthians 6:19-20. What effect do the following words have on you?

"Or do you not know that your body is the temple of the Holy Spirit...?"

"Who is in you, whom you have from God...?"

And what does 1 Corinthians 3:16 also say about your "temple"?

Because the body of the individual believer is the Spirit's temple, you must pay careful attention to it. You must...

- *Guard yourself*—Based on Proverbs 4:23-27, how can you better guard your...

    ...heart?

    ...mouth?

    ...lips?

    ...eyes?

    ...path?

    ...ways?

    ...feet?

- *Walk in righteousness*—How can you better guard your walk based on the commands and warnings from Proverbs 4:14-15?

• *Avoid sexual sin*—Read 1 Corinthians 6:13-20. Why is sexual sin so wrong?

• *Fill your "temple"*—What does God say about holiness in your life as a woman in Titus 2:3?

Your Body Is Not Your Own

Continuing on in our look at 1 Corinthians 6:19-20, what effect do these words have on you?

"And you are not your own?"

"For you were bought at a price."

And what does 1 Corinthians 6:13 also say about your body?

Your Body Was Bought with a Price

Consider again this truth: "For you were bought at a price." What do these scriptures say that price was?

1 Peter 1:18-19—

Ephesians 1:7—

You Are to Glorify God in Your Body

Continuing on in our look at 1 Corinthians 6:19-20, what effect do these words have on you?

"Therefore glorify God in your body and in your spirit..."

"Which are God's."

I hope you enjoyed the little walk-through of the allegorical house. By all means, find a copy of the entire story and read it for yourself. But for our purposes here, follow through on this exercise:

The study—What changes must you make in your reading literature?

The dining room—How can you better nourish your soul?

The living room—Are you neglecting to enter this room as often as you should? And what about today? Have you yet met with Christ?

The workroom—Are you whiling away your time by majoring on the minors, or are you producing something grand—a masterpiece—for your Lord?

The rec room—How do your recreational activities measure up?

The bedroom—Are you keeping yourself holy in body and in spirit? Please explain your answer.

The hall closet—Have you cleared out your hall closet of secret sins…or is there something you need to take care of?

Beloved, God's will for your life is that your body be…

pure	"a vessel for honor,
protected	sanctified and
productive	useful for the Master,
prepared	for every good work."

—2 Timothy 2:21

Now…what will you do?

Looking at Your Life

Please read the "Looking at Life" section in your book again. As you consider the management of your busy life in the light of the contents of this chapter, what actions do you plan to take to live out God's plan for your physical life...

...just for today?

...just for this week?

...just for this month?

...just for this year?

...for life?

5

Ten Disciplines
for Managing Your Body
Part 1

...glorify God in your body...
—1 Corinthians 6:20

 Begin this lesson by reading the chapter in *Life Management for Busy Women* titled "Ten Disciplines for Managing Your Body, Part 1." Note here any new truths or challenges that stand out to you.

There's no doubt that God has given us much to do for Him. If you are married, loving and caring for your husband requires your energy. The same goes for children. And every woman has a home to maintain. Plus many women have jobs. So what is the solution? Our ten disciplines will take us a long way down the road of greater health and energy so we can better manage all the areas of life God's way.

Ten Disciplines for Managing Your Body

1. *Pray for a healthy body*—You'll notice that the first three disciplines for your body involve the spiritual life. As we noted in the first section of the book, the spiritual life affects the physical life. And, since we should pray about every area of our lives, we should pray for healthy bodies. Daily thanksgiving for good health continues to reinforce our dependence and trust in God. Health is not guaranteed in Scripture, but a healthy body can assist in the management of all the areas of our lives.

   Look now in your Bible at the apostle John's prayer in 3 John 2. Give God thanks for your health, and then why not pray for your spiritual life to be vibrant...and that your physical life would match it? (Check here when done.) _____

2. *Acknowledge sin*—Read Psalm 32:3-4 and itemize the physical grievances David suffered when he failed to acknowledge his sin.

   By contrast, what did David experience when he confessed his sin in verses 5 and 11?

   For another account of David's physical suffering due to unconfessed sin, read Psalm 38:1-10. Note any new difficulties.

39

What was the turning point for David in verse 18?

Is there any sin you are allowing to go unconfessed? Or is there any sin you are treating lightly, thinking it doesn't matter, that it won't make a difference in your life...and possibly your health? Why not decide along with David to declare your sin and mourn over it? Why not follow the admonition in 1 John 1:9 to confess your sin? What does Proverbs 28:13 say you will experience as a result? And what does it say will happen to you if you don't?

3. *Walk by the Spirit*—Read through Galatians 5:16-21. What fact does verse 17 give us about the conflict between the flesh and the Spirit?

Now list those "works of the flesh" in verses 19-21 that have to do with the body.

What does the Bible give as a solution to our tendency to sin (verse 16)?

(And, as a bonus question, what fruit of the Spirit do you spot in verses 22-23 that would help you in the management of your body?)

4. *Discipline your body*—According to 1 Corinthians 9:27, what was the passion of Paul's heart when it came to his body and why?

What advice does the Bible give us as women for disciplining our bodies in...

...1 Timothy 3:11?

...Titus 2:3?

And what advice does 1 Corinthians 10:23 add to help us in our disciplines?

And 1 Corinthians 10:31?

Can you point to any area in your physical life that is out of control? How would the implementation of these biblical guidelines help you to better manage your body God's way?

5. *Exercise regularly*—The only time physical exercise is mentioned in the Bible is in 1 Timothy 4:8. What does this verse say...and in contrast to what?

Can you name three or four benefits that you know a "little" exercise would definitely bring your way?

Now, for a look at a woman who "exercised," see Proverbs 31:17. What do you learn here about this remarkable woman? And, as you read verse 16, note what provided her an opportunity to exercise.

An illustration...and a challenge—Throughout the Old Testament, the nation of Israel was responsible for the upkeep of the temple. Amazingly, in times of spiritual decline, the temple was allowed to fall into disrepair. Then, in times of spiritual revival, the temple was meticulously maintained (see 2 Kings 22:1-5).

Dear one, like that physical temple of old, your body is the temple of God (see again 1 Corinthians 6:19). And like the Israelites' temple, how you take care of your temple is an indicator of your spiritual condition. So... what is the condition of your temple? Answer the question in your own words.

Looking at Your Life

Please read the "Looking at Life" section in your book again. As you consider the management of your busy life in the light of the contents of this chapter, what actions do you plan to take to live out God's plan for your physical life...

...just for today?

...just for this week?

...just for this month?

...just for this year?

...for life?

6

Ten Disciplines
for Managing Your Body
Part 2

…glorify God in your body…
—1 CORINTHIANS 6:20

 Begin this lesson by reading the chapter in *Life Management for Busy Women* titled "Ten Disciplines for Managing Your Body, Part 2." Note here any new truths or challenges that stand out to you.

Before we look at five additional disciplines that will help you to manage the physical area of your life as a busy woman, list the five we studied in the previous lesson.

1.   4.

2.   5.

3.

Five Additional Disciplines for Managing Your Body

6. *Seek proper sleep and rest*—When it comes to sleep and rest, we tend to fall on one end or the other of the spectrum. On the passive end, what does Proverbs 6:9-11 tell us?

And Proverbs 19:15?

And Proverbs 20:13?

For the ideal balance in a woman's life, what do we learn from Proverbs 31:27?

I meet many haggard, run-down, burned-out women whose lives are simply out of balance. And usually for one of two reasons. The demands at home are truly taxing. There are babies, preschoolers, teens, and a surplus of responsibilities that cannot be neglected. It's true that such busy-ness accompanies a variety of seasons in a woman's life.

But I also meet women who are exhausted, worn out, and lifeless because they stay up on-line literally half the night. They are the queens of the Internet! They "chat" away, browse, surf, and shop to their hearts' content. On and on their Internet pursuits go, and on and on the night goes. And then they wake up (late!) in the morning to stagger to the computer and start all over again! The same could be said of the many women who read or watch television or movies half the night. They are simply spending their expensive, hard-won energy on the wrong things.

How much better to instill the discipline of going to bed at a reasonable hour. So here's a discipline—pick a bedtime hour that will give you the sleep and rest you need for your busy life, and then head toward bed an hour earlier. By the time you wash your face, brush your teeth, put on your pj's, turn down the bed, and read a few minutes, you'll be ready to have lights-out at the hour you planned on.

Now, dear one, which end of the spectrum do you tend most to live on—the lazy end...or the late-night activity end? And what will you do to discipline yourself toward the ideal, toward being a healthy, bright-eyed, energetic, busy woman whose one desire is to live out God's plan with passion and purpose?

7. *Watch what you eat*—Take a minute to write down a few of the important things you already know the Bible says about food and eating habits.

• *A lesson from Daniel*—Now let's look at the life of Daniel. First, scan through his story in Daniel 1:1-21. How is Daniel's heritage described in verse 3?

How is Daniel described in verse 4?

What was the king's plan for Daniel's life (verse 5)?

And how did Daniel respond (verse 8)?

What test was set up for Daniel and his three friends (verses 12 and 13)?

And what was the result of the test period (verse 15)?

In the end, what did the king find to be true of Daniel and his three companions (verse 20)?

47

• *A lesson from Jonathan*—As I said in our lesson, food is God's way of fueling the body. Scan Jonathan's story in 1 Samuel 14:24-31. What happened to Jonathan when he ate the honey (verses 27 and 29)?

And what was the condition of the people who had not eaten (verses 28 and 31)?

We didn't cover this important fact in our chapter, but what did the people of Israel do because they were so hungry (verse 32), and what was the bottom line regarding their actions (verse 33)?

• *A lesson from Proverbs*—What was the prayer of the wise man of Proverbs 30:8-9?

What do Daniel's and Jonathan's experiences and the prayer from Proverbs teach you about the importance of watching what you eat? Also list a few changes you plan to make regarding your eating habits.

8. *Keep a schedule*—No one can disagree that the life of Christ was planned, organized, and carried out according to a Divine master plan. Jesus had a schedule and a routine. For instance, what do we learn about His schedule and routine in…

...Luke 4:16?

...John 18:2?

Jesus and His schedule—Hear now these descriptive words from another:

> Jesus was ever conscious of His timetable. "I must work the works of Him that sent Me..." (John 9:4 KJV). On His last journey, we see Him headed for Jerusalem (Luke 9:51). He knew death was near, but He still had work to do. He preached in 35 towns and villages in Galilee, Samaria, Perea, and Judea. He planned the itinerary so He would arrive in Jerusalem in time for the Passover—to die on schedule in accordance with the 70-weeks prophecy of Daniel 9. He planned ahead for the Last Supper. He planned for His disciples to continue His mission. And at the end He reported to His Father that He had accomplished His plan (John 17:4). When they came to arrest Him, He offered no resistance; His hour had come! They had attempted to arrest Him before and even stone Him, but He always escaped. Why? Everything went according to plan.[3]

You and your schedule—Now for you, dear heart. God has a plan for your life and He means for you to live it

49

out, *and* to live it out with passion and purpose! So far
we've covered the spiritual and physical areas of your
life. Now, make a schedule for today and for this week
that includes God's plan and your desires for both
areas. (Check here when done.) _____ Be prepared to
share about any major changes.

9. *Take care of your appearance*—Look now at 2 Corinthians
   4:16. What is said here about…

   …the inner man?

   …the outer man?

   Also when it comes to taking care of our appearance,
   what is God most interested in according to…

   …1 Timothy 2:9-10?

   …1 Peter 3:3-4?

   Using the scriptures below, describe…

   …Sarah (Genesis 12:11)

   …Rebekah (Genesis 24:16)

…Rachel (Genesis 29:17)

…Esther (Esther 2:15)

…the Proverbs 31 woman (Proverbs 31:22)

None of us is as beautiful as any of the women on the roll call above (due to the ravages of deterioration of the earth and the human body over time). But there are things we can do to better our appearance. Can you name a few?

10. *Commit to a lifelong pursuit of discipline*—Now it's time to do a "verb" exercise. Mark out the verbs in the following verses. (And be careful—some of them have more than one verb!)

   1 Corinthians 9:26—

   Philippians 3:13-14—

   Colossians 1:23—

   1 Timothy 6:12—

   2 Timothy 2:3—

   2 Timothy 2:5—

2 Timothy 4:5—

2 Timothy 4:7—

Hebrews 12:1—

Now, think about these vigorous acts of those who went before us and also the commands to give our all. Consider, too, the life of one such as J. Oswald Sanders. Note the message these saints are sending to you about a life-long pursuit of discipline. Then read below how God means for *you* to live out discipline in *your* daily life.

> We must not be led to believe that the disciplines are for spiritual giants and hence beyond our reach, or for contemplatives who devote all their time to prayer and meditation. Far from it. God intends the disciplines of the spiritual life to be for ordinary human beings: people who have jobs, who care for children, who must wash dishes and mow lawns. In fact, the disciplines are best exercised in the midst of our normal daily activities.[4]

Looking at Your Life

Please read the "Looking at Life" section in your book again. As you consider the management of your busy life in the light of the contents of this chapter, what actions do you plan to take to live out God's plan for your physical life…

…just for today?

…just for this week?

…just for this month?

…just for this year?

…for life?

7

Managing Your Marriage

This is my beloved, and this is my friend.
—SONG OF SOLOMON 5:16

 Begin this lesson by reading the chapter in *Life Management for Busy Women* titled "Managing Your Marriage." Note here any new truths or challenges that stand out to you.

I described a little bit about what the days of the lives of my family members were like before I began to apply God's principles and guidelines to my marriage, family, and home life. Now take a few minutes to briefly describe a normal day in your home. Then we'll look at God's guidelines and see how we can improve on our little bit of heaven on earth!

God's Guidelines for Marriage

Help your husband—Look at Genesis 2:18. What was the problem and what was the solution?

Then look up the word *helper* in a dictionary. Note its meaning here and then jot down three ways you could help your husband each and every day.

Follow your husband—Look at Ephesians 5:22-24. What is God asking of wives...and more specifically, what is He asking of you, if you are married?

Respect your husband—Look at Ephesians 5:33. Note God's message to wives. Then note several little things you can do immediately to show your respect for your husband.

Love your husband—Look at Titus 2:4. Then think of several ways you can begin to lavish love on your "beloved."

Ten Disciplines for a Meaningful Marriage

1. *You shall center your life on the Lord*—Step 1 in any relationship is to go back to your #1 relationship with God. When *you* are walking with the Lord and nurturing your relationship with *Him*, things seem to improve in your relationship with *him*, your husband. How are you doing on both fronts? Is there anything you need to do to center your life on the Lord?

2. *You shall pray for your husband*—Look up Matthew 6:21. Then stop right now as you're working this lesson and pray for your husband. Pray about his walk with the Lord, his responsibilities, his problems at work, his hobbies and interests, all of the many things that make him him! Then create a special prayer page or prayer notebook just for him. Now you're set up for praying for him daily! (Check here when done.) _____

3. *You shall know your roles*—Write out "God's Four Words for Wives" here. How do you plan to remember these "words" each day? How do you plan to practice these "words" each day? And how do you plan to pray about these "words" each day?

4. *You shall study your mate*—I mentioned earlier the many things about your husband that make him him. Name at least three of those unique things now. Then do as Romans 12:10 (please see) advises and honor your husband by showing him respect and giving him preferential treatment, especially in these specific areas.

5. *You shall be a servant*—Look at Matthew 20:28. Do you see your life role as one of being a servant to all, especially to your husband? Take a minute to answer this question. Then think back to your role of helper (Genesis 2:18). How can you serve and help your husband today?

6. *You shall follow your husband's leadership*—Revisit Ephesians 5:22-24. Then, once again, let's begin with a little thing. In what little way or in what little area can you choose to follow your husband's leadership today? Share your answer below, and then begin to move up the scale to the large and larger issues of life.

7. *You shall make sure your husband is #1*—Read through the scriptures about *leaving* and *cleaving* (Genesis 2:24; Mark 10:7-8; Ephesians 5:31). Is there any person, place, or thing you are failing to leave behind or make secondary so that you can cleave to your husband as the #1 passion in your life? What adjustments must you make to live out God's plan for your marriage?

8. *You shall talk things over*—How would you rate your abilities in this all-important area of communication? Are you one who seeks to communicate...or one who seeks to win? Are you one who listens...or one who does most of the talking? Give your answers, then learn an important lesson from Socrates!

> Once a young man came to the great philosopher Socrates to be instructed in oratory. The moment the young man arrived, he began to speak, and there was an incessant stream for some time.
>
> When Socrates could get in a word, he said, "Young man, I will have to charge you a double fee."
>
> "A double fee, why is that?"
>
> The old sage replied, "I will have to teach you two sciences: first, how to hold your tongue, and then how to use it."[5]

9. *You shall heed a few "don'ts"*—Take a look at these scriptures that give wives a few *do's* and *don'ts* (Proverbs 12:4; 19:13; 27:15; 31:11-12). Can you think of others to add to the list? Now, are you guilty on any counts? What will you do to avoid the *don'ts?*

10. *You shall make each day fun*—To begin this assignment, read Psalm 118:24. What does this verse have to say about a biblical perspective on each and every day? (And did you note the determination? The choice?) Now, what can and "will" you do today to make sure it is a day filled with fun and rejoicing?

Your better management of your marriage can start right now. Today! As you follow God's guidelines, develop the disciplines that make for a better marriage, and pray, then, dear one, you'll find yourself in need of a journal just to keep track of the manifold blessings that will come your way! For as long as God allows you to enjoy your marriage partner, live out His principles so that you *and* your precious husband will be abundantly blessed. May you never be too busy to manage your marriage God's way.

Looking at Your Life

Please read the "Looking at Life" section in your book again. As you consider the management of your busy life in the light of the contents of this chapter, what actions do you plan to take to live out God's plan for your marriage…

…just for today?

…just for this week?

…just for this month?

…just for this year?

…for life?

8

Managing Your Children

Behold, children are a heritage from the LORD,
the fruit of the womb is His reward.
—PSALM 127:3

 Begin this lesson by reading the chapter in *Life Management for Busy Women* titled "Managing Your Children." Note here any new truths or challenges that stand out to you.

Do you have children, dear one? Then you know how needy we mothers are. Childraising is a huge responsibility and the challenges are daily—indeed almost minute by minute! But childraising is a lifework that lives on and on. So let's see what God has to say about managing a lifework…His way.

God's Guidelines for Mothering

Teach your children—Visit Deuteronomy 6:6-7 again, as well as Proverbs 1:8, 6:20, and 31:1. Then answer these questions.

Who is to do the teaching?

Who are they to teach?

What are they to teach?

How are they to teach?

When are they to teach?

Where are they to teach?

Train your children—Two scriptures help us to assume God's role of training our children. What do they say?

Proverbs 22:6—

Ephesians 6:4—

Love your children—According to Titus 2:4, what are the older women to teach the younger moms?

Is there anything you could use help with in this department?

Do you know an older woman who can help you?

Prize your children—Look at Psalm 127:3 and Psalm 113:9. What should our attitude be toward our children and our role as mothers?

Now look at these women from the Bible and note their attitudes:

Sarah—Genesis 21:6-8

Rebekah—Genesis 25:21

Rachel—Genesis 30:1

Hannah—1 Samuel 1:11

Elizabeth—Luke 1:5-7,11-13,24-25

So…what is your attitude toward your children? Are any adjustments needed? Name them…and begin praying *now!*

Ten Disciplines for Mothering

1. *You shall center your life on the Lord*—Turn to Deuteronomy 6:6 again. Before we can affect the heart of our child, whose heart is it that must first be on fire? Whose heart is it that must first be filled with a love for God and a knowledge of His Word?

   Now, what is the temperature of your heart, dear one? We've already spent three chapters in our book on the spiritual area of our lives. Are you beginning to see how *God's Word* at the center of *your* heart is at the heart of it *all?* What's happening (or not happening) in your relationship with God flavors all that you do, every single role and goal. So answer honestly. Then pray about how to turn up the heat (or, in the words of Chef Emeril, to "kick it up a notch!").

2. *You shall model true godly character*—As you think about godly mothers like Samuel's mother (Hannah), Moses' mother (Jochebed), and Timothy's mother (Eunice), how does your character measure up? Is what you are modeling day in and day out a true picture of Christian commitment? Or, put another way, are there any areas of hypocrisy or weakness, any areas that need improvement, that need strengthening? Again, be honest. Then go another step and write out what you plan to do about it.

3. *You shall pray for your children*—Write out what James says about passionate prayer in James 5:16. And while you're at it, substitute the word "mother" in the place of the word "man."

Now, how would you rate the "fervency factor" of your prayers for your children? (And, of course, be honest.) Do changes need to be made?

4. *You shall be there*—Is your heart-cry "home, sweet home" and "family, sweet family"? And does your presence "there" at home match your heart-cry? Look back at your calendar for the past few weeks. Were you gener-

ally home at night? When the children came home from school? What did you discover?

Spend some time in fervent prayer if you need to. Ask God for His wisdom about how you can "be there" more often.

5. *You shall take your children to church*—You and your church are a team when it comes to teaching and training your children. Look again at your calendar. Was church attendance for your family a priority? The Bible exhorts us not to forsake the assembling of ourselves together (Hebrews 10:25), and that includes taking our children to church. Are there serious changes that must be made? If so, what will you do?

6. *You shall choose your children above all other people and pursuits*—Your children are to be a passion and a priority—a *top* priority!—in your life. (You can see it for yourself in Titus 2:4.) Is there any person, place, or thing (other than your husband, of course!) that you are allowing to hold a higher-priority position in your schedule and your heart than your dear, God-given children? What adjustments must you make to live out God's plan for your mothering?

7. *You shall discipline your children*—What two kinds of parents are depicted in Proverbs 13:24? And what are the evidences of each?

What, then, is God's message to you as one of His parents? (And if you need advice in this area, please talk with an older mother in the church.)

8. *You shall be your children's #1 encourager*—Life is hard... even for your children. So be their chief cheerleader. Point out their character qualities, their noble deeds, their areas of improvement. Who better than you? What does Proverbs 12:25 have to say to you about this role of encourager?

9. *You shall nurture your marriage*—The family is a unit designed by God. And your children benefit by seeing a healthy marriage. Even if things are not ideal, you can still bless and instruct your children and set and create a pleasant home environment by living out your role. And if that seems difficult, remember Colossians 3:23. In fact, write it out here. (And don't forget your most powerful weapon of all—prayer!) What changes must you make to nurture your marriage?

10. *You shall make each day fun*—Just as with your husband, make each day under your roof fun for your children. Read again Psalm 118:24. What does this verse have to say about a biblical perspective on each and every day? (And did you note the determination? The choice?) Now, what can and "will" you do today to make sure it is a day filled with fun and rejoicing? (And remember, too, the joyful mother of children in Psalm 113:9!) May such be your heart!

Looking at Your Life

Please read the "Looking at Life" section in your book again. As you consider the management of your busy life in the light of the contents of this chapter, what actions do you plan to take to live out God's plan for your role as a mother...

...just for today?

...just for this week?

...just for this month?

...just for this year?

...for life?

9

Managing Your Home

She watches over the ways of her household.
—PROVERBS 31:27

 Begin this lesson by reading the chapter in *Life Management for Busy Women* titled "Managing Your Home." Note here any new truths or challenges that stand out to you.

I don't know where you are on "the homemaking scale." But I do know that God's Word gives us specific guidelines, instructions, and help for this major and daily area of life.

God's Guidelines for Homemaking

Build your home—Everyone lives somewhere. Therefore, every woman has a home. What do these verses say and picture about the wise woman and her home?

Proverbs 9:1—

Proverbs 14:1—

Proverbs 24:3-4—

Now, what steps in daily planning and organizing and work do you think are necessary to accomplish the "building" of a home and its atmosphere?

Watch over your home—Now look at Proverbs 31:27. What two clues does this verse give about how this wise woman accomplished the "building" of her house?

Manage your home—Take a look at the problem in 1 Timothy 5:13-14. How do you think the busy-ness of homemaking keeps women off the streets and out of "trouble"?

Love your home—Read Titus 2:3-5. Note especially what is said about the importance of the home in verse 5. Now rate yourself on the "*love* of homemaking scale."

How do you think a greater love for your home would empower you to do the tasks that must be done there?

And how do you think you can begin to nurture a greater love for home and homemaking? (And I'll give you the first hint—pray. Pray for your heart, your home, and your attitude!)

Ten Disciplines for Managing Your Home

1. *You shall be dedicated to managing your home*—Once again, Jesus' words in Matthew 6:21 come to mind. Write them out below. Then ponder how they would apply to your dedication to your homemaking and home management.

2. *You shall be a woman of prayer*—Continuing on with Matthew 6:21, how would spending the "treasure" of your time and prayer effort on your home and homemaking make a difference? As one of my prayer principles states, "You cannot hate the person—or thing—you are praying for." Also, "You cannot neglect the person—or thing—you are praying for."

3. *You shall be aware of the basics*—Do take a few minutes to read through Proverbs 31:10-31. Jot down a list of the many basic areas (and relationships) she managed and cared for.

4. *You shall be on a schedule*—Oh, the beauty of a schedule! What a relief it is to know *what* you need to do and *when*. And Step 1 is to have a schedule. So make an ideal schedule now...for today and for this week. Then put it in a prominent place...like on the kitchen counter. (Check here when done.) _____

5. *You shall be organized*—Walk through your home and jot down on a master note pad or 3" x 5" cards what needs to be better organized in each room. Then decide on a plan for getting organized. Do you need to read a book? Do you need to purchase any items such as shelves, caddies, or file cabinets? Do you need to get help from someone who is highly organized? Don't forget to include these steps in your master plan. (Check here when done.) _____

6. *You shall be there*—There's only one way to work out your plans, schedule, and dreams—you must be there, be at home. So, with schedule in hand, see how many outings, evening activities, and get-togethers you can lop off and clear out of your overly busy schedule. Saying *no* to some things means you can say *yes* to others. This act is called "redeeming the time" (see Ephesians 5:16). This, dear one, is how you and I buy back time, time for making our dreams come true at home. Write out

what you plan to say *no* to for the next week. (And, I warn you, wondrous things will begin to happen as you repeat this exercise for life. In fact, it will be *life-changing!*)

7. *You shall be the best*—What was said about the woman in Proverbs 31:29?

Beloved, this is her eternal epitaph! Wouldn't you like the same said of you by your husband, children, and all who know you (see verses 28-31)? Therefore be ever growing, ever excelling! What can—and will—you do this week to excel in the management of your home?

8. *You shall be reading*—Reading is the single most important method for growing in knowledge and for learning new skills. Of course, your Bible is always the primary source for the information that will guide your life forever and in all areas. But beyond that, you can be educated, instructed, stimulated, and motivated in every area of your life—even in the area of home management—by reading. As you've probably heard before, "reading is to the mind what exercise is to the body." Now, name a time management book you are reading or plan to obtain so that you can better live out God's

plan for you at home. To illustrate our need to read, what does Proverbs 15:14 say along these lines?

9. *You shall be frugal*—Our next section will be about managing the financial area of our lives. For now, though, I am asking you to own your role and assignment from God to pay attention to money matters. And frugality is a part of that role.

10. *You shall be creative*—Read again and note the Proverbs 31 woman's creativity in...

verse 13—	verse 19—
verse 14—	verse 21—
verse 16—	verse 22—
verse 18—	verse 24—

These verses describe this wonderful woman's creativity.[6] Sure, it was work! All creative effort is work. But don't you think her heart was humming with joy as she expressed her intellectual and artistic abilities at her workplace called home (see verse 13)? Now, how does the thought of expressing your creativity motivate you in your homemaking?

As we leave the study of this vital section of our lives, think again about the place where you live, the place you call *home*. You and I have little control over most of the events of our lives. But we do have a measure of control over the atmosphere and the order and the smooth running of our homes. You see, what's inside our doors and under our roofs is *our* sphere. It's *our* place. By and large, it's a sphere and a place we build, watch over, manage, and love. So why shouldn't we dive in and do it with great passion and purpose? Why not write out a prayer for your home and your management of it?

Looking at Your Life

Please read the "Looking at Life" section in your book again. As you consider the management of your busy life in the light of the contents of this chapter, what actions do you plan to take to live out God's plan for your home…

…just for today?

…just for this week?

…just for this month?

…just for this year?

…for life?

10

God's Guidelines
for Your Money

Seek first the kingdom of God and His righteousness,
and all these things shall be added to you.
—MATTHEW 6:33

 Begin this lesson by reading the chapter in *Life Management for Busy Women* titled "God's Guidelines for Your Money." Note here any new truths or challenges that stand out to you.

So far you and I have learned that every area of our lives is a stewardship. All that we have and are is given to us by God and is to be managed for Him and lived out in a way that glorifies Him. We've looked at the fact that we are to be faithful stewards of our spiritual lives, of our bodies (remember—we are not our own!), and of our marriages, families, and home lives. Well, hang on to your hat (and your pocketbook)! We are also to be stewards of our finances. Let's look now at some guidelines related to our money.

You Are a Steward

To begin our study, write out 1 Corinthians 4:2.

Then look up the word *steward* in your dictionary and write out the definition.

What do these verses teach us about our money and everything else we have?

Job 1:21—

Psalm 49:17—

Ecclesiastes 5:15—

1 Timothy 6:7—

Briefly restate the points Jesus made in His parable about the importance of stewardship in Matthew 25:14-30.

Assessing your stewardship—In this chapter of your book I asked you to think through what you have that God has entrusted to you. Do that now, realizing that each blessing translates into a stewardship.

Meet someone who managed her money well—As usual, the Proverbs 31 woman gives a picture of all virtues, including that of taking care of the business of money management. What do these verses from Proverbs 31 indicate about her financial care?

verse 11—	verse 20—
verse 14—	verse 24—
verse 16—	verse 27—
verse 18—	verse 31—

What example does she set for you?

God Will Provide for All Your Needs

What strong messages do we receive regarding God's provision for His children from...

Matthew 6:25-34—

Philippians 4:19—

Psalm 37:25—

2 Corinthians 9:8—

• *Assessing your trust in the Lord*—Here's a two-part exercise.

—First, make a list of what you perceive to be the needs in your life, any needs.

—Then read through the beloved Psalm 23. What are the basic promises you can count on? (And did they cover all your needs?)

• *Meet someone who failed to trust in God's provision*—Poor Eve! Read her story now in Genesis 3:1-6. (Check here when done.) _____

The next time you doubt God's provision for you, how can Hebrews 11:1 help?

You Are Called to Contentment

—*Contentment is learned*—Look at Philippians 4:11-12. What did Paul *learn* in…

…verse 11?

…verse 12?

And what did Paul *know* according to…

…verse 12?

How do Paul's learned lessons and his example encourage you to greater faith and contentment?

—*Contentment is required when you have much*—What words did Paul use that indicate he had had much at periods in his life?

—*Contentment is required when you have little*—And what words did Paul use that indicate he had had little at periods in his life?

I call these two conditions "the school of plenty" and "the school of want." Dear one, which school do you consider yourself to be in at this time, and what is Paul's challenge to you from verses 11 and 12?

—*Contentment is not based on your present circumstances*—According to John 16:33, what did Jesus say about the condition of our lives on this earth?

And where is our peace to be found?

—*Contentment is based on the person of God*—Scan again Psalm 23. What is the true source of all that we need?

• *Assessing your contentment*—What do these scriptures teach us about discontentment?

Philippians 4:6-7—

Hebrews 13:5-6—

James 4:1-3—

Are there any corrections you need to make...or any promises you need to remember?

• *Meet someone who was truly content*—Read the story of the dear Shunammite woman in 2 Kings 4:8-17. How does she show us "the rare jewel of Christian contentment"?

As you can see, dear one, your life is *not* about money or fortune or success. No, your life is about God and godliness, about living in a way that honors and glorifies *Him*. And how you gain and manage and use your money should benefit *others*—your family, your church, your society, your nation.

Dear sister, be thankful for God's financial blessings, but also be alert to the effect money can have on your heart, on your spiritual life, and on the spiritual life of your family. Yes, you can master and manage your finances. But beware—don't let them master you!

Looking at Your Life

Please read the "Looking at Life" section in your book again. As you consider the management of your busy life in the light of the contents of this chapter, what actions do you plan to take to live out God's plan for your finances...

...just for today?

...just for this week?

...just for this month?

...just for this year?

...for life?

11

Ten Disciplines
for Managing Your Money

For where your treasure is, there your heart will be also.
—MATTHEW 6:21

 Begin this lesson by reading the chapter in *Life Management for Busy Women* titled "Ten Disciplines for Managing Your Money." Note here any new truths or challenges that stand out to you.

Jesus warned us, "You cannot serve God and mammon." However, we are called upon to manage our "mammon." So here are ten ways to get started.

Ten Disciplines for Managing Your Money

1. *You shall not be in debt*—See for yourself what Proverbs 22:7 says about being in debt.

Look, too, at Romans 13:8.

What ways can you as a woman, wife, mother, and homemaker think of to help reduce any indebtedness? Write them down and then share them with others.

(And, as a bonus question, how do you think prayer could make a difference in your spending habits?)

2. *You shall not spend more than you make*—How does someone get into debt? Usually by violating this discipline—they are spending more than they make! I know these are hard questions, but is this your situation? Or are any of the danger signals mentioned in our book true of your finances?

Drawing upon some of the ideas presented in this lesson, what can you begin to do to turn things around? Think of at least three immediate actions.

3. *You shall not buy on credit*—It's time to look at Proverbs 22:27. What is its common-sense warning?

   How do *you* hold the line on credit? Or, if you fall on the debt side of the credit issue, what will you do to begin holding the line? And once you've answered this question, try this "easy credit plan"—100 percent down with nothing to pay each month!

4. *You shall not covet what others have*—Rather than looking to others, to our neighbors, and to the world to set our standards, what did Jesus say to do instead in Matthew 6:33?

   What can the love of money lead to, according to 1 Timothy 6:10?

   And what was the apostle Paul's example to the Ephesian elders in Acts 20:33?

Finally, what did God say in the Ten Commandments in Exodus 20:17?

5. *You shall not love money*—Copy 1 Timothy 6:10 here.

Then read through Matthew 6:19-21. What solution does Jesus offer us to safeguard against a love of money, and what warning does He give in verse 24?

6. *You shall give regularly to your church*—You don't have to answer these questions in your book…only in your heart. When was the last time you gave to your church, and what was the amount? This information will reveal quite a bit about your heart! (Remember—where your treasure is *is* where your heart is!)

What do these scriptures say about your giving?

—1 Corinthians 16:2

—2 Corinthians 9:6

—2 Corinthians 9:7

Now here's another question you can answer in your heart...and in your checkbook—decide what you will give to your church this next Sunday. And if you're married, be sure to talk it over with your husband. By the time you go to bed Saturday evening, have your check written out and tucked into your Bible.

7. *You shall give generously*—Revisit the Proverbs 31 woman, specifically verse 20. How many ways do you see her giving generously?

Revisit the Shunammite woman in 2 Kings 4:8-10. How did she give generously?

And now meet Dorcas in Acts 9:36-39. How did she give generously?

Dear one, continue to pray daily about these disciplines. But pray earnestly for this one! Pray for a giving heart and for God's guidance as you seek to become a better steward of His resources. Then, who knows how many people you will bless, beginning with your own dear family. Who knows...?

8. *You shall know your financial condition at all times*—Ignorance is not bliss when it comes to your knowledge of your finances. No, a good steward would never be ignorant of his situation. Financial management is not something we do once in a while. It's something we do faithfully and passionately...so that we stay out of debt, pay the bills on time, and give to the church regularly. So...what is your financial condition? (And again, you don't need to write this down. Just *know!*) And if you need to, ask your husband. You'll never know what you must do to *improve* your financial condition until you *know* what that condition is.

As the head home manager, you probably handle larger amounts of money than you're aware of! So if you know things are tight (or tilted!), you can hold back. But Step 1 is to *know*.

9. *You shall have a reserve*—We know we're not to "lay up... treasures on earth" (Matthew 6:19). But a wise money manager has a little extra...for emergencies, for disasters, and for unknown needs and opportunities. I'm thinking again of the Proverbs 31 woman. What does verse 16 say?

That's it! An opportunity came along...and this wise woman had a reserve and was therefore able to take advantage of it. Do you have a "rainy day fund"?

10. *You shall practice self-control*—Write out again God's command in Galatians 5:16 and note again His fruit of self-control in verse 23. The woman who masters herself is not only free, but debt free! Never forget that the Christian lifestyle is one of self-denial, self-control, and self-restraint.[7]

As we close our study on taking care of the business of our finances, here's a little "test" to help you determine the power money has in your heart and your life. It comes to us under the banner of...

Money Must Be Managed
or It Will Manage You

1. Do you think and worry about money frequently?

2. Do you give up doing what you should do or would like to do in order to make more money?

3. Do you spend a great deal of your time caring for your possessions?

4. Is it hard for you to give money away?

5. Are you in debt?

How much better it is
to let God be your Master![8]

Looking at Your Life

Please read the "Looking at Life" section in your book again. As you consider the management of your busy life in the light of the contents of this chapter, what actions do you plan to take to live out God's plan for your finances...

...just for today?

...just for this week?

...just for this month?

...just for this year?

...for life?

12

God's Guidelines
for Your Friendships

A friend loves at all times, and a brother is born for adversity.
—PROVERBS 17:17

 Begin this lesson by reading the chapter in *Life Management for Busy Women* titled "God's Guidelines for Friendships." Note here any new truths or challenges that stand out to you.

If you're like most women, your busy days are filled with people. Think through your typical day. I shared mine… and now it's your turn. About how many people are involved? Who makes up your immediate family? Do you have other family nearby? How about best friends? Your neighbors? What are your involvements at the church? At work?

Friendships with Family

Marriage—We've looked at it before, but what does Genesis 2:18 say about your relationship with your husband?

Look again, too, at Titus 2:4. What does this verse say about your relationship with your husband?

• *The Shulamite and King Solomon*—Some day soon read all of the beautiful, exquisite love story presented in Song of Solomon. But for now, write out 5:16.

As I asked in your book, could you sing this same "song" about your feelings toward your dear husband? Why or why not? And if not, how can you change your heart attitude toward your husband?

• *Elizabeth and Zacharias*—Describe the age and the situation of this faithful-to-God couple (Luke 1:7).

In spite of their trials, what is said of this couple in verse 6?

• *Sarah and Abraham*—What was God's first request of this faithful-to-God couple (Genesis 12:1)?

And how did they respond (verse 4)? Also note Abraham's age at this time.

How many years passed from the time this couple obeyed God until they had a child (Genesis 21:5)?

And how many more years passed until Sarah's death (Genesis 23:1)?

Also briefly note how the lifestyle of this twosome is described in Hebrews 11:8-16.

- *Your marriage*—What tips on marriage can you gather from these couples to apply in your own marriage? (Choose at least one from each couple.)

Children—Look again at Titus 2:4. What does this verse say about your relationship with your children?

Now revisit the list of people you said make up the days of your life on the opening page of this lesson. How many of them are mentioned in Titus 2:3-5?

And what does this say to you about the top priority billing God means for your children to take in your heart, your time, and your life?

- *Moses' mother*—Here's an amazing mother! What distressing event came her way (Exodus 1:22–2:3)?

And yet what opportunity did God arrange (2:5-10)?

In time, this woman's three children—Moses, Aaron, and Miriam—became the leaders of God's people!

- *Samuel's mother*—Here's another amazing mother. What distressing event came her way (1 Samuel 1:2,11,20, 24-28)?

In time this woman's child became the leader of God's people!

- *Solomon's mother*—How did Bathsheba passionately refer to her son in Proverbs 31:1-2 as she taught him?

In time this son became a king over God's people and the wisest man who ever lived before Jesus Christ.

- *Timothy's mother and grandmother*—What role did this godly female twosome have in their Timothy's life (2 Timothy 1:5; 3:15)?

In time Timothy grew up to become the apostle Paul's friend, companion, and co-laborer.

LIFE MANAGEMENT FOR BUSY WOMEN GROWTH AND STUDY GUIDE

• *John the Baptist's mother*—We've already met Elizabeth, the barren wife of Zacharias. What blessing was finally hers (Luke 1:57)?

Be sure you read Luke 1:57-80 to find out about Elizabeth's son John, the passionate forerunner and messenger of the Messiah, Jesus Christ.

• *Your children*—How do these dedicated, devoted, and grateful mothers inspire you as the mother of your children? Or, put another way, what lessons can a woman apply to her role as a mother?

Parents and siblings—What a blessing family is! But nurturing family relationships requires commitment and effort. What does the Bible say about your relationship with your parents (Ephesians 6:2-3 and Exodus 20:12)?

Now, how can you better honor your parents (and don't forget your husband's parents!)?

And how can you better nurture relationships with your siblings (and don't forget their mates!)?

Friendships Within the Family of God

As you think about the deep friendship between David and Jonathan (read 1 Samuel 18:1-3), think, too, about your relationships with your "best" friends as you read through these questions.

• Do you share a common love for the Lord, or are you "unequally yoked" in your passion for serving God?

• Do you share a common love for one another, or is the give-and-take tilted?

• Do you want the best *for* each other...or do you want something *from* each other?

• Do you bring out the best in each other...or do you get what you want?

• Do you encourage one another in the Lord...or is your friendship centered on trivial pursuits?

These are hard questions. But your friendships are vital to your relationship with God. Your friends are either pulling you down (away from God) or pulling you along and/or up (toward God). (And, dear one, you are doing the same for them!) What do these scriptures have to say about the company you are to keep?

—1 Corinthians 15:33

—Proverbs 22:24-25

As you pray about your friendships, remember the pattern set by David and Jonathan—they desired the best for each other, they encouraged the best in each other, and they gave their best to each other.

Friendships Outside the Church

Do you pray regularly for your friendships with non-Christians? That, dear one, is your primary ministry to them! Your prayers will focus your friendship on what's truly important—their knowledge of Jesus Christ! Set up prayer pages for them now…and, of course, pray! (Check here when done.) _____

Looking at Your Life

Please read the "Looking at Life" section in your book again. As you consider the management of your busy life in the light of the contents of this chapter, what actions do you plan to take to live out God's plan for your friendships…

…just for today?

…just for this week?

…just for this month?

…just for this year?

…for life?

13

Ten Disciplines
for Managing Your Friendships

Do not forsake your own friend.
—PROVERBS 27:10

 Begin this lesson by reading the chapter in *Life Management for Busy Women* titled "Ten Disciplines for Friendships." Note here any new truths or challenges that stand out to you.

Did you enjoy the roll call of faithful friendships at the beginning of this chapter? Obviously, friendship (a real one, that is) has many facets and many layers to it...even to the depth of risking your life! Hopefully these disciplines will help you be a better friend.

Ten Disciplines for Friendships

1. *Be loyal*—What two different scenarios do we see lived out in friendships in these verses?

   —Proverbs 18:24

   —Psalm 41:9 and 55:12-14

   How can you keep your allegiance toward others?
   —Proverbs 17:9

   —Proverbs 17:17

   —Proverbs 27:10

   Have you failed on any of these guidelines? If so, how can you improve yourself as a friend?

2. *Do not keep score*—Look up 1 Corinthians 13:5. Do you know what "love thinks no evil" means? And more than that, are you guilty of keeping score in any relationships with family or friends?

How does 1 Corinthians 12:26 say you should respond to your friends instead?

And Romans 12:15?

And what is the principle from Luke 6:35?

Now, how can you be a better family member and friend?

3. *Be respectful and sensitive*—Here are a couple of fun verses with a forceful message! What is that message?

—Proverbs 25:17

—Proverbs 27:14

How do you show respect and sensitivity to your best friends? Do corrections need to be made?

4. *Be honest...and be attentive*—How are you in the honesty department? Are you a flatterer? Or are you a spiritual cheerleader? What is your desire? Please explain.

And when honest communication is called for, do you speak the truth in love and after much prayer (Ephesians 4:15) as a faithful friend (Proverbs 27:6)?

And do you listen, take to heart, appreciate, and thank your friends in turn when they are honest with you? How do you normally respond?

5. *Be careful with the opposite sex*—What did you think of this section? Of the thought of "holy jealousy"? Of a no-tolerance level of flirtations between couples? And further, how can you erect "an invisible barrier" around you and your marriage partner?

6. *Seek to witness in your encounters*—How do you measure up on the following ministries to all those you encounter?

—*The ministry of friendliness.* Do you pay attention to your encounters? Ask your heart. Then make a list of what you can give by way of friendliness to those who cross your path.

—*The ministry of encouragement.* Giving encouragement is a decision. It's a choice we make. And what choice does Proverbs 3:27 say we should make?

Make a list of what you can say by way of encouragement to those who cross your path.

—*The ministry of witnessing.* We never know what is accomplished in a person's heart when we dare to open our mouths and speak of the Lord. What threefold process could be going on, according to 1 Corinthians 3:7-8? And what is your role?

Begin to pray daily for opportunities to "plant" and "water" in the souls of others. In fact, stop now and ask God for His heart and His help.

7. *Be an incessant encourager*—Look again at David and Jonathan's friendship in 1 Samuel 23:16. What role did Jonathan have in David's life at that time?

   Now, what encourages you?

   And how can you encourage others?

   Why not adopt this people-principle as your own? "In every encounter make it your goal that the other person is better off for having been in your presence."

8. *Prioritize your friendships*—Do the exercise I suggested in this section of your book. Just who are the people you spend the bulk of your time with?

   And is your time with them spent in meaningful ways, especially if these people are not Christians?

And does it appear that your priorities (Titus 2:4) are in order based on who you spend the bulk of your time with?

9. *Nurture your friendships*—Obviously, we nurture our friendships with family first (Titus 2:4). But beyond that, what are some things you do to nurture your friendships with others?

And what more can you do to imitate Paul in Philippians 1:3-8?

10. *Pray for your friends*—My life prayer verse is Ephesians 6:18. Write down its instructions now.

Now, do you need to be a better friend, to pray more faithfully for your friends? Explain how you will make such a desire a reality. Be sure you have a prayer page for each "friend."

We've covered a lot about our precious friendships…and at the same time much has been left unsaid. Dear one, just pray to keep a sensible perspective and a strict rein on the time you spend with others outside of your family. There's a place for the fun and learning and interaction that takes place when women get together. Social interaction with other women is a needed part of our life. But always remember that our higher calling is to manage our life so that we live out *God's* plan with passion and purpose. That plan includes nurturing a vital and passionate relationship with Him and passionately living out our roles as a wife, mother, and home manager. After these pursuits, *then*, and only then, we seek to be the best friend we can be to the many other people in our wonderful, packed, busy life!

Looking at Your Life

Please read the "Looking at Life" section in your book again. As you consider the management of your busy life in the light of the contents of this chapter, what actions do you plan to take to live out God's plan for your friendships…

…just for today?

…just for this week?

…just for this month?

…just for this year?

…for life?

14

God's Guidelines
for Your Mind

*Finally, brethren, whatever things are true...noble...
just...pure...lovely...of good report, if there is any virtue
and...anything praiseworthy—[think] on these things.*
—PHILIPPIANS 4:8

 Begin this lesson by reading the chapter in *Life
Management for Busy Women* titled "God's Guidelines for Your Mind." Note here any new truths or
challenges that stand out to you.

Did you ever think about the fact that your mind is one
of the world's most powerful computers? And it's *yours!*
But that reality also means that you must manage it, discipline it, and direct it. That's a tall order, isn't it? But we
have help and guidelines from the Bible.

God's Guidelines: What to Think...and Not Think

As we step into this most important section of our study on managing your busy life *and* your busy mind, begin by writing out Philippians 4:8 here. When you're done, be sure you underline God's final command at the end of the verse.

Next, read through the questions in your book that define each of the qualities our thoughts are to measure up to. Under each quality, write out the question that challenged you most or brought you a new understanding of the standard God sets for our thoughts. Then briefly tell why.

• *Is it true?*—

• *Is it noble?*—

• *Is it just?*—

• *Is it pure?*—

• *Is it lovely?*—

• *Is it of good report?—*

• *Is it praiseworthy?—*

• *Is there any virtue?—*

Beloved, we are to think on *these* things! What difference do you think thoughts like these would make in your...

...outlook on life?

...attitude toward people?

...mental health and emotional stability?

Our thoughts should be like an evergreen—Think now of this image of an evergreen tree and describe it in your own words. Then write out its message to you regarding your thought patterns.

Our thoughts should be like a cathedral—Think now of this image of a cathedral and describe it in your own words. Then write out its message to you regarding your thoughts.

Our thoughts should be disciplined—Write out each of these scriptures and note how following their instructions would change and help your thoughts to match up to God's standards.

—Colossians 3:1

—Colossians 3:2

Now that you better understand God's guidelines for your thoughts and the need to discipline them, what three steps or changes will you make immediately to "think on these things"?

—

—

—

God's Guidelines: What to Do...and Not Do

Problem-solving—Name a problem you are facing and list three actions you can take to determine a solution.

Decision-making—Name a decision you must make and list three actions you can take to move you toward a wise decision that helps you to better live out God's plan for your life.

Planning—Name an upcoming event or activity on your calendar and spend 20 minutes in initial planning. Determine the *who, what, where, when,* and *how*'s of making your event or activity a success. Then write out below the benefits of your planning session, how this exercise brought your future event into the present, and the satisfaction you enjoyed in knowing that real steps of action are being taken toward something that is an important part of your life.

What do these verses from Proverbs remind us and teach us by way of illustration about our planning?

6:6-8—(illustration)

16:3—

16:9—

20:4—

20:18—(illustration)

21:5—

Organizing—Pick the worst *problem* area in your home. *Decide* what you must and will do about it. *Plan* a way of *organizing* it. Then *schedule* a 15-minute slot for working on it. Check here when done. (By the way, did you notice the involvement of all five exercises?) _____

As an added exercise, what major project did King Solomon plan, organize, and schedule in 1 Kings 4:7?

Scheduling—Here's where realities collide in every busy woman's life. We can think, pray, dream, desire, consult, plan, and visualize. But finally the actual work must be slotted into your packed calendars. So, look at the results of your problem-solving, decision-making, planning, and organizing exercises, and then place them on your schedule. Check here when done. _____

As an added exercise, note two of the Proverbs 31 woman's scheduling slots—

Proverbs 31:15—

Proverbs 31:18—

And here's one more exercise. It's an eye-opener... and well worth your time. It points out to us that whether our problems are large or small, the same mental exercises help us to manage and handle them God's way. How did the brave and wise Abigail deal with a very serious and life-threatening situation? Can you pinpoint the five mental exercises involved in her dilemma in 1 Samuel 25?

Dear one, every one of these exercises is a discipline. But the ultimate discipline is your follow-through. This section of the chapter is titled "What to Do...and Not Do." Therefore, if you do these exercises and fail to follow-through, you are allowing what you *didn't* do to spoil what you determined you needed to do. And, my friend, this could seriously affect your ultimate desire to live out God's plan and purpose for your life. So don't fail to dive in and actually *do* what you've decided to do, planned to do, and scheduled to do.

Now here's one final exercise for you to do. Share here how David Brainerd's passionate quote regarding the use of time spoke to your heart and your life.

Looking at Your Life

Please read the "Looking at Life" section in your book again. As you consider the management of your busy life in the light of the contents of this chapter, what actions do you plan to take to live out God's plan for your mind...

...just for today?

...just for this week?

...just for this month?

...just for this year?

...for life?

15

Ten Disciplines
for Managing Your Mind

And do not be conformed to this world,
but be transformed by the renewing of your mind.
—ROMANS 12:2

Begin this lesson by reading the chapter in *Life Management for Busy Women* titled "Ten Disciplines for Managing Your Mind." Note here any new truths or challenges that stand out to you.

Give your mind to Christ
that you may be guided by His wisdom.[9]

Ten Disciplines for Managing Your Mind

1. *Be reading your Bible*—Read Philippians 4:8 again. How do you think reading your Bible will help you to think the kinds of thoughts this verse advocates?

   Now read Romans 12:2. How do you think reading your Bible will help you to...

   ...not be conformed to this world?

   ...be transformed?

   ...renew your mind?

2. *Be memorizing*—What does Psalm 119:11 say memorizing God's Word accomplishes? (And don't you think such an accomplishment would help you to better live out God's plan for your life?!)

123

Read through Deuteronomy 31:9-13. What is this scene meant to accomplish (verses 12-13)?

According to Ephesians 6:16-17 and 1 Peter 5:8-9, what is another advantage of memorizing Scripture?

Beloved, can you think of *any* reason you couldn't memorize one Bible verse every month? Now, what will your verse for this month be?

3. *Be developing*—What "plan" do you find for your mind in 1 Peter 2:2?

And in 2 Peter 3:18?

What was Paul's "plan" in Philippians 3:10?

Develop by setting goals—One of my favorite proverbs is Proverbs 15:14. What does it say your goals should be when it comes to the use of your mind?

Develop by reading—And how does Proverbs 15:14 apply to the goal and habit of reading?

Develop your professional skills—Do you agree or disagree that because you represent Jesus Christ on your job, you should be the best you can be on your job? Please explain...and then evaluate the message you are sending regarding Christianity.

What can or should you do to develop your professional skills?

And do you agree or disagree that your marriage, family, and home take top billing and top priority over a job? (Revisit Titus 2:3-5 to see where your family and home fits into God's plan.) Are there any changes you need to make? Write them out here.

4. *Be preparing*—All that you learn can be shared with others. Even if what you are learning serves only to improve and perfect you as a Christian, then others are blessed. We'll spend the next two lessons on your ministry to others. But at this time, what does 1 Corinthians 12 say about God's plan for your ministry and about your need to prepare for it?

Verse 7—

Verse 11—

Verse 18—

How exciting it is to know that God has gifted us to do something for other believers! Therefore...be preparing!

5. *Be sharing*—I shared a number of statistics with you about how sharing and interacting with what you are learning increases *your* knowledge. But, dear one, *others* benefit when you share what you are learning. What is one of your God-given assignments, according to Titus 2:3-4?

6. *Be challenged*—I also shared with you that I keep a time management book on my night stand. I've probably already read a hundred time management books, but I want to remain challenged in this vital area. Reading a few minutes a day on this essential subject is a tiny investment when laid next to the payoff of learning new skills and sharpening old ones. Another challenge I place before myself is reading through the Bible each year. Yes, I've read the Bible…many times. But I continue to challenge myself. And, you guessed it—I continue to discover new truths and grow in a multitude of ways. Plus the passion level of my life is most definitely heightened! Now, in what areas of life would you like to achieve greater growth and knowledge? And what goals can you set for yourself to ensure that you are challenged to do so?

7. *Be varied*—Jot down some of the many ways you purposefully learn and grow. Can you think of others you'd like to cultivate? (And what's keeping you from attempting them?)

8. *Be continuing*—In our lesson on "Ten Disciplines for Managing Your Body," we committed to a lifelong pursuit of discipline. And that goes for a lifelong pursuit of continuing to grow mentally and intellectually! How does Paul's "purpose statement" in Philippians 3:12-14

cause you to desire to continue in your efforts to grow and serve God to the "max" and to the end?

9. *Be reviewing*—What did the apostle Peter desire in 2 Peter 1:12-13?

And in 2 Peter 1:15?

And what did the apostle Paul charge his protégé Timothy to do in 2 Timothy 2:14?

Now how can you s-t-r-e-t-c-h what you've already learned (along with stretching your mind!) by reviewing? (And remember, it's a discipline. You may need to write out some things on 3" x 5" cards or spiral pads...and remember to carry them with you. You may need to remind yourself to turn the radio *off* when you're driving the car so you can think and review. You may need to purchase a new version of the Bible and read it through. You may need to revisit some favorite books. Or take a refresher course. Or brush up on some dying skill. Or purchase a journal so you can begin to record...and review...what you are learning. Be sure and note how you will review.)

10. *Be selective*—As you focus on the future, spend time thinking about who you are in Christ and how you would like to affect others with your life. Then think about how you must manage your life and your mind so that you can (by God's grace!) make such a contribution. Dear one, your time is so precious that it simply cannot be wasted...not even a precious minute. (Remember... "just a tiny little minute, but eternity is in it.") So it's your call—what do you choose to do?

Looking at Your Life

Please read the "Looking at Life" section in your book again. As you consider the management of your busy life in the light of the contents of this chapter, what actions do you plan to take to live out God's plan for your mind…

…just for today?

…just for this week?

…just for this month?

…just for this year?

…for life?

16

God's Guidelines
for Your Ministry

Having gifts then differing according to the grace
that is given to us, let us use them.
—ROMANS 12:6

 Begin this lesson by reading the chapter in *Life Management for Busy Women* titled "God's Guidelines for Your Ministry." Note here any new truths or challenges that stand out to you.

We're almost there! We've almost completed our tour of the seven areas that basically make up our lives as Christian women. God has entrusted us with multiple roles and responsibilities to manage. It's obvious, isn't it, that we have a lot to do. (No wonder we're so busy!) And now it's time to consider one final area, our ministry in the body of Christ.

As a believer, you possess spiritual gifts that are meant to be ministered to other believers in the body of Christ. Let's look at some guidelines about this.

Our Giftedness to Serve the Lord

• We'll attempt a list of the gifts later, but for now, what does Romans 12:6 say about these gifts?

• And 1 Corinthians 12:7?

• And Ephesians 4:7?

• And 1 Peter 4:10?

• Write a summary statement of what these scriptures teach about spiritual gifts. Also note the common threads you observed in these verses.

• Once again, what is a steward, and what does a steward do? What then must you do to be a good, responsible steward of your spiritual gifts?

Our Array of Service to the Lord

As you read and research the spiritual gifts, you can't help but notice the exciting variety of gifts. But, as 1 Corinthians 12:11 states, each and every one of them is empowered by the same Holy Spirit.

Some of the gifts—As you read through these scriptures, jot down the various gifts mentioned.

Romans 12:6-8—

1 Corinthians 12:8-10—

1 Peter 4:11—

Three of the gifts—According to theologian Charles Caldwell Ryrie, three of the spiritual gifts are not only gifts, but are commanded of all Christians. He writes that "three of the [spiritual] gifts probably all

Christians could have and use if they would. They are ministering, giving, and showing mercy (Romans 12:7-8)."[10] Now, think of three ways you can minister each of these graces to others each and every day. (And don't forget to begin with those under your own roof!)

Serving—

Giving—

Showing mercy—

Some who ministered their gifts—I hope you found the service of the many women of the Bible inspiring. Evidently God did, for He has preserved their deeds of service forever in His Word. Now, let's take a closer look at them for ourselves. Read the scriptures and then jot down what each woman did and the thing that impressed you most about her.

• The women who supported Jesus—Luke 8:2-3

• Mary and Martha—Luke 10:38-39

• The women who remained at the cross—Luke 23:49–24:10

• John Mark's mother—Acts 12:12

• Lydia—Acts 16:40

• Phoebe—Romans 16:1-2

• Priscilla—1 Corinthians 16:19 and Acts 18:24-26

• The widows—1 Timothy 5:10

• The older women—Titus 2:3-5

Commenting on the precious women of the Bible who have gone before us, Dr. Herbert Lockyer remarks,

> In the annals of the Early Church, women are...notable for their spiritual devotion, fidelity in teaching the Word of God, and sacrificial support of God's servants. Their faith and prayers were mingled with those of the apostles...and all through the Christian era, the church owes more than it realizes to the prayers, loyalty and gifts of its female members.[11]

How can *you*, dear one, follow in the footsteps of these busy female saints? How can *you* minister your gifts, your prayers, and your support to the body of Christ? Don't leave this section without listing three steps you could take and purposing to take them! This is an area of life management that Christ does not intend for you to neglect!

1.

2.

3.

Now, what is it that tends to keep you from serving the Lord? Be honest.

Our Growth for Serving the Lord

As you roll up your ministry sleeves and get busy serving the Lord and His people, your areas of spiritual giftedness will emerge. It is in the *doing* that we *discover*. So look for these indicators.

Joy—what service brings you the most joy?

Fruit—what service blesses others most?

Affirmation—what are others saying about your service?

Invitation—what are others asking you to do?

Glorification—what service gives God the most glory?

137

Looking at Your Life

Please read the "Looking at Life" section in your book again. As you consider the management of your busy life in the light of the contents of this chapter, what actions do you plan to take to live out God's plan for your ministry...

...just for today?

...just for this week?

...just for this month?

...just for this year?

...for life?

17

Ten Disciplines
for Managing Your Ministry

As each one has received a gift, minister it to one another,
as good stewards of the manifold grace of God.
—1 PETER 4:10

 Begin this lesson by reading the chapter in *Life Management for Busy Women* titled "Ten Disciplines for Managing Your Ministry." Note here any new truths or challenges that stand out to you.

I hope you feel like the pieces of your life are falling into place. Also as we finish with a few more disciplines, I hope you're thinking differently about your busy-ness. Most women are busy...but many are busy with secondary things. Hopefully our study has pointed out what the few primary things in life are that require and deserve our precious time!

Ten Disciplines for Managing Your Ministry

1. *Develop "five fat files"*—Did you enjoy the thought of having five fat files? I have to admit I got excited all over again. There's never a dull day when you know there is something you want to learn and purposefully seek to learn it. As you take time to think and pray about what your five fat files might contain, what comes to mind?

   File and topic #1—

   File and topic #2—

   File and topic #3—

   File and topic #4—

   File and topic #5—

Now, check here when you've obtained five file folders. And, if you've filled in the information above, go ahead and label your files. (Check here when you are done.)

———

2. *Determine your spiritual gifts*—Begin working your way through the series of questions in your chapter about "asking." Persevere...and don't get discouraged. Remember, for the rest of your life you'll be seeking, sharpening, and serving others in the body of Christ with your spiritual gifts. Two general rules for determining your gifts are:

   • stay in God's Word—how can you be faithful each day?

   • stay busy—what can you do in service this week?

3. *Develop your spiritual gifts*—Can you think of three ways you can purposefully seek to develop your spiritual gifts? They can be as varied as volunteering in a ministry...to meeting with someone who is doing what you would like to learn to do; from enrolling in a training class to looking for men and women in the Bible who ministered the spiritual gifts you have. Take time to think through this assignment, and write your answers on the next page. And you are welcome to write down more than three!

—

—

—

4. *Do pray for ministry opportunities*—It's easy to become
   overly involved in interests and activities that have
   nothing to do with being a Christian or with ministering to other Christians. Prayer turns our hearts to
   our church and to the needs of God's people.

   What did Paul exhort all Christians to do in Ephesians
   6:18?

   And what ministry did Epaphras have in Colossians
   4:12?

   Now, what will you do today to begin praying for ministry opportunities and praying *as* a ministry?

5. *Do accept the challenge to grow*—Beloved, you will never lack for ministry...if you grow! As we work our way through this section on the joys and responsibilities of spiritual growth and ministry, consider how you tend to spend your time. Is it spent in worthy pursuits? Is it spent growing in Christ? Is it spent developing yourself and your spiritual gifts for greater ministry? Is it spent with others in mind? As we noted, our problem isn't really a lack of time. Our problem is the management of *self* so that we use our time in the good, better, and best ways. I'm glad you're working this lesson, because reading the book *Life Management for Busy Women* is a giant growth step. And so is working through this growth and study guide. Now determine to do one thing tomorrow to accept the challenge to grow. What will it be? And while you're at it, what will it be each day for the next week?

6. *Do allow yourself to be stretched*—Look now at Philip's ever-expanding ministry. First read Acts 6:1-5. What was the problem, and what was the solution?

Who was selected, and why?

Now read Acts 8:5-12. Describe Philip's ministry as recorded here.

Philip's ministry stretched even further. Read Acts 8:26-40. Where do we find him now, and what was the impact of his ministry?

Now turn to Titus 2:3-4. What is the ministry of the "older women" in these verses?

Many believe that these older women were like those older widows described in 1 Timothy 5:10. What growth and ministry had occurred in their lives to qualify, stretch, and prepare them for their ministry as spiritual instructors, according to 1 Timothy 5:10?

And what was their teaching curriculum (Titus 2:4-5)?

Now, *if* a younger woman listens, learns, and implements what the older women are teaching, what might she realistically be doing in the future in the area of ministry, according to Titus 2:3-5?

7. *Do support others in ministry*—Look first at Philippians 4:2-3. What was evidently going on, and what did Paul ask of the leaders in the church?

Now look at 1 Corinthians 12:14-25. Briefly distill this description of the body of Christ as related to the spiritual gifts.

Beloved, there is *no* room in the body of Christ for jealousy, pettiness, arguing, and troublemaking in the church! If we are to live out God's plan for our lives, one of our purposes is to minister...and to support others in ministry. How can you assist others who are serving the Lord Christ and His people?

8. *Do pray for your pastors and leaders*—Our church leaders are to hold a high position of respect in our hearts. What instructions are given to us in...

...1 Thessalonians 5:12-13?

...Hebrews 13:7?

...Hebrews 13:17?

We noted that praying is a ministry. And your ministry in your church can begin right this minute as you begin to faithfully pray for your pastors and leaders. Check here when you've set up a prayer page for these esteemed officers in your church._____ (And don't forget to pray...now!)

9. *Don't neglect your family for ministry*—This should go without saying, but unfortunately things can get out of whack! I'm often asked when I began writing. And I always answer, "after both of my daughters married." As long as my girls were unmarried, I wanted them to know they had a home they could come to at any time. (And, believe me, they did...along with all their friends!) Yes, I did teach and disciple in my home church. But those ministries occurred around my daughters' lives. To add the rigors of writing was another whole dimension! But I always had a saying that guided me as I prayed about ministry—*never sacrifice your family on the altar of ministry*. Is your family and ministry ratio, or balance, a healthy one? Do any changes need to be made?

10. *Decide that ministry is for life*—What lifelong ministry and ministry pursuit does God give to you and me as His women in Titus 2:3-5?

Two scriptures never fail to encourage me when it comes to our calling to minister for life—Philippians 3:13-14 and 1 Corinthians 15:58. As you look at them and we close off our study about this glorious and useful way to spend our time and our lives, I pray that you, too, are encouraged to commit yourself to a lifetime of selfless service to our Lord and to His people. (And while you're at it, why not write out your commitment?)

Looking at Your Life

Please read the "Looking at Life" section in your book again. As you consider the management of your busy life in the light of the contents of this chapter, what actions do you plan to take to live out God's plan for your ministry…

…just for today?

…just for this week?

…just for this month?

…just for this year?

…for life?

18

Managing Your Time...
and Your Life

See then that you walk circumspectly, not as fools but as wise,
redeeming the time....Therefore do not be unwise,
but understand what the will of the Lord is.
—EPHESIANS 5:15-17

 Begin this lesson by reading the chapter in *Life Management for Busy Women* titled "Managing Your Time...and Your Life." Note here any new truths or challenges that stand out to you.

Congratulations for making it to the end of the journey! Well done! I'm sure you've enjoyed seeing firsthand what God's Word has to say about your life—every feature and facet of it. You probably met up with some familiar principles along the way, as well as a few new ones. There's certainly no doubt that there is always room for improvement when it comes to time and life management!

As we finish up our study, this final lesson will be used as a time of evaluation and reflection as we recognize yet a few more valuable principles for managing our life God's way and for living out His plan with passion and purpose.

Redeeming Your Time

In your Bible, look long and hard at Ephesians 5:15-17. Specifically note these thoughts...

...walk circumspectly. Look up the word *circumspectly* in your dictionary. Then write this command from God in your own words.

...not as fools. How do you think fools walk through their days?

...but as wise. By contrast, how do you think the wise walk through their days? (And here's a thought— "Minutes are worth more than money. Spend them wisely.")

...redeeming the time. Write out here the definition of "redeeming the time" that was given in your book. Then enjoy the inspiring thoughts in the quote on the next page.

What possibilities are yours? Every new day that dawns is a fresh opportunity: it is like the marble in the quarry waiting for you to chisel out of it some beautiful thing—some lasting monument of purity and grace that shall stand for you when your life on earth is ended. Remember that God gives you the marble to make of it what you will.[12]

...because the days are evil. What did Jesus have to say in Matthew 6:34 about the days of our lives on this earth?

...do not be unwise. This is a command to stop that which is already in progress, to stop becoming foolish. Can you think of any wasteful ways you are spending your time and your life? Can you think of something you need to stop doing (or start doing) to turn a corner toward greater wisdom? Just name one...but make it a big one!

...understand what the will of the Lord is. As one scholar commented, this passage in Ephesians 5 calls for "the end of the self-centered life"[13] After reading the book *Life Management for Busy Women* and working through the growth and study guide, what do you now understand the will of the Lord to be concerning your life?

Guarding Your Time

Now that we know our time is to be redeemed, we must carefully guard it. How do you measure up on these "robbers" of your time...and what are your plans for "guarding" your time against them?

1. Procrastination—

2. Poor planning and scheduling—

3. People not on the plan for the day—

4. Poor delegation—

5. Poor use of the phone—

6. Poring over junk mail and newspapers—

7. Priorities out of whack—

Praying About Your Time...and Your Life

We've covered a lot, haven't we? But just to be sure nothing is forgotten, take time now to review your notes on the seven areas of life that we've focused on in this study and in your book. Jot down the commitments you desire to make in each important area, commitments that will help you to live out God's plan for your life with both passion and purpose. Then commit these decisions to God by taking time to pray about your time and your life. May we never be too busy to live out God's will!

Spiritual life—

Physical life—

Family life—

Financial life—

Social life—

Mental life—

Ministry life—

Living Out God's Plan

Now, for today and every day, use the prayer on the next page to guide you in living out God's plan for your life. And may He richly bless you as you live each day, week, month, and year for Him with great passion and purpose!

A Prayer for Living Out God's Plan

1. *Pray over your priorities*—"Lord, what is Your will for me at this time in my life?"

2. *Plan through your priorities*—"Lord, what must I do today to accomplish Your will?"

3. *Prepare a schedule based on your priorities*—"Lord, when should I do the things that live out these priorities today?"

4. *Proceed to implement your priorities*—"Lord, thank You for giving me Your direction for my day."

5. *Purpose to check your progress*—"Lord, I only have a limited time left in my day. What important tasks do I need to focus on for the remainder of the day?"

6. *Prepare for tomorrow*—"Lord, how can I better live out Your plan for my life tomorrow?"

7. *Praise God at the end of the day*—"Lord, thank You for a meaningful day, for 'a day well spent,' for I have offered my life and this day to You as a 'living sacrifice.'"

$\mathscr{L}$eading a Bible Study Discussion Group

$\mathscr{W}$hat a privilege it is to lead a Bible study! And what joy and excitement await you as you delve into the Word of God and help others to discover its life-changing truths. If God has called you to lead a Bible study group, I know you'll be spending much time in prayer and planning and giving much thought to being an effective leader. I also know that taking the time to read through the following tips will help you to navigate the challenges of leading a Bible study discussion group and enjoying the effort and opportunity.

The Leader's Roles

As a Bible study group leader, you'll find your role changing back and forth from *expert* to *cheerleader* to *lover* to *referee* during the course of a session.

Since you're the leader, group members will look to you to be the *expert* guiding them through the material. So be well prepared. In fact, be over-prepared so that you know the material better than any group member does. Start your study early in the week and let its message simmer all week long. (You might even work several lessons ahead so that you have in mind the big picture and the overall direction of the study.) Be ready to share some additional gems that your group members wouldn't have discovered on their own. That extra insight from your study time—or that comment from a wise Bible teacher or scholar, that clever saying, that keen observation from another believer, and even an appropriate joke—adds an element of fun and keeps Bible study from becoming routine, monotonous, and dry.

Next, be ready to be the group's *cheerleader*. Your energy and enthusiasm for the task at hand can be contagious. It can also stimulate people to get more involved in their personal study as well as in the group discussion.

Third, be the *lover*, the one who shows a genuine concern for the members of the group. You're the one who will establish the atmosphere of the group. If you laugh and have fun, the group members will laugh and have fun. If you hug, they will hug. If you care, they will care. If you share, they will share. If you love, they will love. So pray every day to love the women God has placed in your group. Ask Him to show you how to love them with His love.

Finally, as the leader, you'll need to be the *referee* on occasion. That means making sure everyone has an equal opportunity to speak. That's easier to do when you operate under the assumption that every member of the group has something worthwhile to contribute. So, trusting that the Lord has taught each person during the week, act on that assumption.

Expert, cheerleader, lover, and referee—these four roles of the leader may make the task seem overwhelming. But that's not bad if it keeps you on your knees praying for your group.

A Good Start
Beginning on time, greeting people warmly, and opening in prayer gets the study off to a good start. Know what you

want to have happen during your time together and make sure those things get done. That kind of order means comfort for those involved.

Establish a format and let the group members know what that format is. People appreciate being in a Bible study that focuses on the Bible. So keep the discussion on the topic and move the group through the questions. Tangents are often hard to avoid—and even harder to rein in. So be sure to focus on the answers to questions about the specific passage at hand. After all, the purpose of the group is Bible study!

Finally, as someone has accurately observed, "Personal growth is one of the by-products of any effective small group. This growth is achieved when people are recognized and accepted by others. The more friendliness, mutual trust, respect, and warmth exhibited, the more likely that the member will find pleasure in the group, and, too, the more likely she will work hard toward the accomplishment of the group's goals. The effective leader will strive to reinforce desirable traits" (source unknown).

A Dozen Helpful Tips

Here is a list of helpful suggestions for leading a Bible study discussion group:

1. Arrive early, ready to focus fully on others and give of yourself. If you have to do any last-minute preparation, review, re-grouping, or praying, do it in the car. Don't dash in, breathless, harried, late, still tweaking your plans.

2. Check out your meeting place in advance. Do you have everything you need—tables, enough chairs, a blackboard, hymnals if you plan to sing, coffee, etc.?

3. Greet each person warmly by name as she arrives. After all, you've been praying for these women all week long, so let each VIP know that you're glad she's arrived.

4. Use name tags for at least the first two or three weeks.

5. Start on time no matter what—even if only one person is there!

6. Develop a pleasant but firm opening statement. You might say, "This lesson was great! Let's get started so we can enjoy all of it!" or "Let's pray before we begin our lesson."

7. Read the questions, but don't hesitate to reword them on occasion. Rather than reading an entire paragraph of instructions, for instance, you might say, "Question 1 asks us to list some ways that Christ displayed humility. Lisa, please share one way Christ displayed humility."

8. Summarize or paraphrase the answers given. Doing so will keep the discussion focused on the topic; eliminate digressions; help avoid or clear up any misunderstandings of the text; and keep each group member aware of what the others are saying.

9. Keep moving and don't add any of your own questions to the discussion time. It's important to get through the study guide questions. So if a cut-and-dried answer is called for, you don't need to comment with anything other than a "thank you." But when the question asks for an opinion or an application (for instance, "How can this truth help us in our marriages?" or "How do *you* find time for your quiet time?"), let all who want to contribute.

10. Affirm each person who contributes, especially if the contribution was very personal, painful to share, or a

quiet person's rare statement. Make everyone who shares a hero by saying something like "Thank you for sharing that insight from your own life," or "We certainly appreciate what God has taught you. Thank you for letting us in on it."

11. Watch your watch, put a clock right in front of you, or consider using a timer. Pace the discussion so that you meet your cut-off time, especially if you want time to pray. Stop at the designated time even if you haven't finished the lesson. Remember that everyone has worked through the study once; you are simply going over it again.

12. End on time. You can only make friends with your group members by ending on time or even a little early! Besides, members of your group have the next item on their agenda to attend to—picking up children from the nursery, babysitter, or school; heading home to tend to matters there; running errands; getting to bed; or spending some time with their husbands. So let them out *on time!*

Five Common Problems

In any group, you can anticipate certain problems. Here are some common ones that can arise, along with helpful solutions:

1. *The incomplete lesson*—Right from the start, establish the policy that if someone has not done the lesson, it is best for her not to answer the questions. But do try to include her responses to questions that ask for opinions or experiences. Everyone can share some thoughts in reply to a question like, "Reflect on what you know about both athletic and spiritual training and then share what you

consider to be the essential elements of training oneself in godliness."

2. *The gossip*—The Bible clearly states that gossiping is wrong, so you don't want to allow it in your group. Set a high and strict standard by saying, "I am not comfortable with this conversation," or "We [not *you*] are gossiping, ladies. Let's move on."

3. *The talkative member*—Here are three scenarios and some possible solutions for each.

   a. The problem talker may be talking because she has done her homework and is excited about something she has to share. She may also know more about the subject than the others and, if you cut her off, the rest of the group may suffer.

   SOLUTION: Respond with a comment like: "Sarah, you are making very valuable contributions. Let's see if we can get some reactions from the others," or "I know Sarah can answer this. She's really done her homework. How about some of the rest of you?"

   b. The talkative member may be talking because she has *not* done her homework and wants to contribute, but she has no boundaries.

   SOLUTION: Establish at the first meeting that those who have not done the lesson do not contribute except on opinion or application questions. You may need to repeat this guideline at the beginning of each session.

   c. The talkative member may want to be heard whether or not she has anything worthwhile to contribute.

SOLUTION: After subtle reminders, be more direct, saying, "Betty, I know you would like to share your ideas, but let's give others a chance. I'll call on you later."

4. *The quiet member*—Here are two scenarios and possible solutions.

   a. The quiet member wants the floor but somehow can't get the chance to share.

   SOLUTION: Clear the path for the quiet member by first watching for clues that she wants to speak (moving to the edge of her seat, looking as if she wants to speak, perhaps even starting to say something) and then saying, "Just a second. I think Chris wants to say something." Then, of course, make her a hero!

   b. The quiet member simply doesn't want the floor.

   SOLUTION: "Chris, what answer do you have on question 2?" or "Chris, what do you think about...?" Usually after a shy person has contributed a few times, she will become more confident and more ready to share. Your role is to provide an opportunity where there is *no* risk of a wrong answer. But occasionally a group member will tell you that she would rather not be called on. Honor her request, but from time to time ask her privately if she feels ready to contribute to the group discussions.

   In fact, give all your group members the right to pass. During your first meeting, explain that any time a group member does not care to share an answer, she may simply say, "I pass." You'll want to repeat this policy at the beginning of every group session.

5. *The wrong answer*—Never tell a group member that she has given a wrong answer, but at the same time never let a wrong answer go by.

> SOLUTION: Either ask if someone else has a different answer or ask additional questions that will cause the right answer to emerge. As the women get closer to the right answer, say, "We're getting warmer! Keep thinking! We're almost there!"

Learning from Experience

Immediately after each Bible study session, evaluate the group discussion time using this checklist. You may also want a member of your group (or an assistant or trainee or outside observer) to evaluate you periodically.

May God strengthen—and encourage!—you as you assist others in the discovery of His many wonderful truths.

Quiet Times Calendar

Jan.	Feb.	Mar.	Apr.	May	June
1	1	1	1	1	1
2	2	2	2	2	2
3	3	3	3	3	3
4	4	4	4	4	4
5	5	5	5	5	5
6	6	6	6	6	6
7	7	7	7	7	7
8	8	8	8	8	8
9	9	9	9	9	9
10	10	10	10	10	10
11	11	11	11	11	11
12	12	12	12	12	12
13	13	13	13	13	13
14	14	14	14	14	14
15	15	15	15	15	15
16	16	16	16	16	16
17	17	17	17	17	17
18	18	18	18	18	18
19	19	19	19	19	19
20	20	20	20	20	20
21	21	21	21	21	21
22	22	22	22	22	22
23	23	23	23	23	23
24	24	24	24	24	24
25	25	25	25	25	25
26	26	26	26	26	26
27	27	27	27	27	27
28	28	28	28	28	28
29		29	29	29	29
30		30	30	30	30
31		31		31	

DATE BEGUN

July	Aug.	Sept.	Oct.	Nov.	Dec.
1	1	1	1	1	1
2	2	2	2	2	2
3	3	3	3	3	3
4	4	4	4	4	4
5	5	5	5	5	5
6	6	6	6	6	6
7	7	7	7	7	7
8	8	8	8	8	8
9	9	9	9	9	9
10	10	10	10	10	10
11	11	11	11	11	11
12	12	12	12	12	12
13	13	13	13	13	13
14	14	14	14	14	14
15	15	15	15	15	15
16	16	16	16	16	16
17	17	17	17	17	17
18	18	18	18	18	18
19	19	19	19	19	19
20	20	20	20	20	20
21	21	21	21	21	21
22	22	22	22	22	22
23	23	23	23	23	23
24	24	24	24	24	24
25	25	25	25	25	25
26	26	26	26	26	26
27	27	27	27	27	27
28	28	28	28	28	28
29	29	29	29	29	29
30	30	30	30	30	30
31	31		31		31

Notes

1. Edith L. Doan, ed., *The Speaker's Sourcebook* (Grand Rapids: Zondervan Publishing House, 1997), p. 32.

2. W. L. Doughty, ed., *The Prayers of Susanna Wesley* (Grand Rapids: Zondervan Publishing House, 1984), pp. 40-41.

3. Mark Porter, *The Time of Your Life* (Wheaton, IL: Victor Books, 1983), p. 127.

4. Richard J. Foster, *Celebration of Discipline—The Path to Spiritual Growth* (San Francisco: Harper Row Publishers, 1978), p. 1.

5. Michael Hodgin, *1001 More Humorous Illustrations for Public Speaking* (Grand Rapids: Zondervan Publishing House, 1998), p. 71.

6. For a verse-by-verse understanding of Proverbs 31, read *Beautiful in God's Eyes—The Treasures of the Proverbs 31 Woman* by Elizabeth George (Eugene, OR: Harvest House Publishers, 1998).

7. Roy B. Zuck, *The Speaker's Quote Book* quoting Bob Jones (Grand Rapids: Kregel Publications, 1997), p. 344.

8. Neil S. Wilson, ed., *The Handbook of Bible Application* (Wheaton, IL: Tyndale House Publishers, Inc., 1992), pp. 422-23.

9. Doan, ed., *The Speaker's Sourcebook*, p. 161.

10. Charles Caldwell Ryrie, *Balancing the Christian Life* (Chicago: Moody Press, 1969), pp. 96-97.

11. Herbert Lockyer, *The Women of the Bible* (Grand Rapids: Zondervan Publishing House, 1975), p. 20.

12. D. L. Moody, *Notes from My Bible and Thoughts from My Library* (Grand Rapids: Baker Book House, 1979), p. 308.

13. G. Campbell Morgan, *Life Applications from Every Chapter of the Bible* (Grand Rapids: Fleming H. Revell, 1994), p. 350.

Personal Notes

Personal Notes

Personal Notes

Personal Notes

Personal Notes

Personal Notes

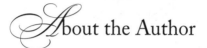

About the Author

Elizabeth George is a bestselling author and speaker whose passion is to teach the Bible in a way that changes women's lives. For information about Elizabeth's books or speaking ministry, to sign up for her mailings, or to share how God has used this book in your life, please write to Elizabeth at:

Elizabeth George
P.O. Box 2879
Belfair, WA 98528

Toll-free fax/phone: 1-800-542-4611
www.elizabethgeorge.com

∾

Books by Elizabeth George

Beautiful in God's Eyes—The Treasures of the Proverbs 31 Woman
Life Management for Busy Women
Life Management for Busy Women Growth and Study Guide
The Lord Is My Shepherd—12 Promises for Every Woman
Loving God with All Your Mind
A Woman After God's Own Heart®
A Woman After God's Own Heart® Audiobook
A Woman After God's Own Heart® Growth and Study Guide
A Woman After God's Own Heart® Prayer Journal
Women Who Loved God—365 Days with the Women of the Bible
A Woman's High Calling—10 Essentials for Godly Living
A Woman's High Calling Growth and Study Guide
A Woman's Walk with God—Growing in the Fruit of the Spirit
A Woman's Walk with God Growth and Study Guide

A Woman After God's Own Heart® Bible Study Series

Walking in God's Promises—The Life of Sarah
Cultivating a Life of Character—Judges/Ruth
Becoming a Woman of Beauty & Strength—Esther
Nurturing a Heart of Humility—The Life of Mary
Experiencing God's Peace—Philippians
Pursuing Godliness—1 Timothy
Growing in Wisdom & Faith—James
Putting On a Gentle & Quiet Spirit—1 Peter

Children's Books

God's Wisdom for Little Boys—Character-Building Fun from Proverbs
(co-authored with Jim George)
God's Wisdom for Little Girls —Virtues & Fun from Proverbs 31
God's Little Girl Is Helpful
God's Little Girl Is Kind